Little Books from A to Z

by Christine E. McCormick
and Jana M. Mason

Illustrated by Deborah K. Reich

D0125100

Good Year Books

An Imprint of Addison-Wesley Educational Publishers Inc.

Acknowledgments
The authors thank Millie Fleming and her kindergarten class for their helpful feedback during the field evaluation of the Little Books.

 Good Year Books

are available for most basic curriculum subjects plus many enrichment areas. For more Good Year Books, contact your local bookseller or educational dealer. For a complete catalog with information about other Good Year Books, please write:

Good Year Books
1900 East Lake Avenue
Glenview, IL 60025

Design: Street Level Studio

I S B N   0-673-57727-9

2 3 4 5 6 7 8 9 - ML - 06 05 04 03 02 01 00 99 98

Table of Contents

    My Little A Book
    My Little B Book

    My Little C Book
    My Little D Book

    My Little E Book
    My Little F Book

    My Little G Book
    My Little H Book

    My Little I Book
    My Little J Book

    My Little K Book
    My Little L Book

    My Little M Book
    My Little N Book

    My Little O Book
    My Little P Book

    My Little Q Book
    My Little R Book

    My Little S Book
    My Little T Book

    My Little U Book
    My Little V Book

    My Little W Book
    My Little X Book

    My Little Y Book
    My Little Z Book

Preface

Little Books from A to Z contains 26 reproducible, easy-to-recite, high-interest Little Books for children who are learning to recognize letters and connect the letters with their primary sounds at the beginning of words. Each book fosters awareness of initial sounds by emphasizing a specific letter. The five-page Little Books, one for each letter of the alphabet, provide an easy-to-remember text with child-friendly supporting illustrations. We're sure you will find that your children will enjoy reciting the Little Books over and over again as they delight in their success at the first steps toward learning to read.

Christine E. McCormick,
Eastern Illinois University

Jana M. Mason,
University of Illinois

Introduction

Letter recognition and the **phonemic awareness** skill of connecting printed letters with their sounds (e.g., the words *milk* and *mop* begin with the same sound /m/, and the letter *m* represents that sound) are widely recognized as important predictors of individual differences in learning to read. *Little Books from A to Z* encourages success with these skills.

Within this book are **26 Little Books**, one for each letter of the alphabet.

Styled upon the **successful format** of *Little Books* (published in 1990 by Good Year Books), *Little Books from A to Z* presents a few words of text on each page with an illustration that clearly depicts the text.

The **simplicity of the text** allows children to recite the text after an introduction and model reading by the teacher. *Little Books from A to Z* is intended to supplement other class activities for the letters and **may be used in any order.** They are intended to be introduced during letter instruction and then given to each child to keep and use at home.

Many easy books on the market, including the aforementioned *Little Books*, emphasize a holistic approach to the early stages of reading. However, *Little Books from A to Z* helps children to begin to realize the **link between a letter and its sound(s)** and fosters skills closely related to systematic reading instruction. For example, each Little Book emphasizes a specific letter sound at the beginning of words. Children are then encouraged to remember the specific words of the text for each book and develop awareness that most of the words in each Little Book begin with a specific letter.

Procedures

Getting Ready for the Lessons

Present *Little Books from A to Z* in the same sequence that you introduce or review the letters of the alphabet. Using a Little Book at the conclusion of your other activities for a letter is probably best, when children can use the book as a **review or culminating activity**. Each book may be introduced to the entire group or to smaller groups of children—for example, as a center activity.

Be sure to preread each Little Book before presenting it to children. You may want to spend a few minutes discussing words from the text that may be unfamiliar to the children before introducing the Little Book to them.

When you are ready to introduce a Little Book, tell children that you have a Little Book for the letter _____ and that they will later be given a copy to keep and use at home. Plan to spend about 10 minutes with each book.

Preparing the Little Books in This Resource for Use

Notice that pages for two Little Books appear on each page in the Little Book section of this resource. This format allows easy photo-copying and assembly of the teacher's and children's copies. **By photocopying a set of six full pages, two Little Books will be formed in their correct sequence.** Remember to make at least one set of Little Books as a group copy for introduction of the books and one copy for each child, if possible.

To prepare the copies, follow these instructions.

1. Remove six perforated pages, which form two complete books, or press the book flat on the copier and copy the six pages.

2. To make more copies of these two Little Books, use these perforated pages or the copied pages as your master, and then copy and collate.

3. Cut the pages horizontally, resulting in two complete books.

4. Staple the left side twice on each book.

You may wish to make an enlarged group copy if you are introducing the Little Book to a group. Laminating this copy will make it sturdier.

Using the Books

Opening

Arrange the children in front of you, in a semicircle if the group is small or in rows if the group is large. Hold the Little Book so that everyone can see it; making an enlarged group copy will make this easier. Begin the lesson by showing the children the title page of the Little Book and saying that you will be helping them to read a book for the letter _____. Then say, "This book's title is *My Little _____ Book*" and underline the words with your finger. Explain that many of the words in this book will begin with the letter _____. You may want to point out that the picture on the title page represents a word that begins with that letter's sound.

Modeling and Tryouts

Read the text aloud to the children in a clear and animated voice. Use your finger to underline the print as you read. After the first reading, the children may have questions about some of the words or pictures. You may want to take a few minutes to talk about what is happening in the "story" or to explain that it's just a fun book for the letter _____.

Then read through the book a second time, again using your voice to animate the "story line" and underlining the text with your finger as you read.

After you have read the book twice, have children read the story with you. If you hear words that do not match the text, you may need to model those words again. Have the children (individually or by row) read a page of the Little Book. Always respond positively to the children's attempts at reading the words.

Closing

Conclude each presentation of a Little Book with a reminder that the story uses words that begin with the letter _____ . You may want to talk about objects in the classroom that begin with the same letter. You may also want to reread a book for a letter already introduced in class.

As you end a session, remind children where the new book will be placed in the classroom so that they can look at it and read it later. Also remind them of your procedure for taking home a copy of the Little Book.

Teacher Tips

1. Accurate reciting of the text is the goal, but children will vary in how quickly they remember the exact words and catch on to the idea that most of the words begin with a specific letter's sound. A positive early literacy experience is the most important outcome of these materials, so provide gentle reminders about the words if children are having difficulty remembering. For example, point to the initial letter of troublesome words, emphasizing the initial sound when you say them.

2. Be sure to make available to the children, in the reading corner or other prominent location, a group copy of all introduced Little Books. Children may then enjoy and practice them along with other books.

3. If at all possible, provide each child with a personal copy of each of the Little Books to use at home. Children will enjoy reciting the books at home and over time will gain increased insight into the link between the letter and its corresponding sound at the beginning of words.

4. Occasional reviewing of previously presented books will help the children remember the words and encourage accuracy. If a particular child or group of children has difficulty remembering the words, you may want to provide extra modeling before they take the books home.

5. Give the children suggestions about how to keep their books in one place at home. Another option is to provide them with a special bag with handles or help them to create a decorated box for their Little Books. Remind children that by the end of the school year they will have a book for each letter of the alphabet.

6. Introducing parents to the goals and purpose of *Little Books from A to Z* is helpful. A sample parent letter is provided on the next page. Be sure that parents realize that the books are meant to be recited and that the children may not remember all of the exact words.

Sample Parent Letter

Date:

Dear Parent/Guardian:

During the year, your child will be bringing home a Little Book for each letter of the alphabet as we study that letter. These books are for your child to keep and use at home. Please help your child find a special bag or box in which to keep the Little Books.

The brief text and matching pictures in the Little Books will help your child remember and recite the words; your child is not expected to actually read the words. These books are intended to be an enjoyable at-home practice for connecting letters to their sounds at the beginning of words.

As you enjoy the books together, answer questions your child may have about the words, but remember that he or she may not remember the words exactly. The most important use of the books is that of fostering a love of reading, as your child becomes increasingly aware of the relationships between letters and their sounds.

Sincerely,

Little Books

from A to Z

My Little **A** Book

My Little **B** Book

1

Ants in pants

1

Bear on bike.

ask for apples. —— **2**

Bird on bear. —— **2**

3

A lot of apples.

3

Bumpity-bump.

Apples, ahhh!

4

Bye-bye bird.

4

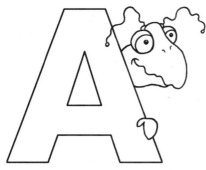

I read my
Little Book to:

1. _____

2. _____

3. _____

I read my
Little Book to:

1. _____

2. _____

3. _____

My Little C _____ Book

My Little D _____ Book

Can you carry

1

Dog digs.

1

a cup and a cake

Duck digs.

3

and a clown and a cat

3

Dinosaur digs.

on a cow?

Dinosaur digs down deep.

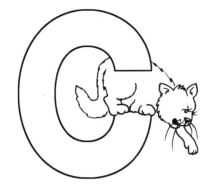

I read my Little Book to:

1. _____

2. _____

3. _____

I read my Little Book to:

1. _____

2. _____

3. _____

My Little E Book

My Little F Book

1

Elephant enters.

1

Five fish

Elephant eats.

2

fry food

2

3

Elephant exits

3

and find forks.

in an elevator.

4

Five fat fish.

4

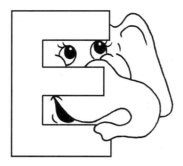

I read my
Little Book to:

1. _____

2. _____

3. _____

I read my
Little Book to:

1. _____

2. _____

3. _____

My Little G Book

My Little H Book

Grandma goat

1

Horse with a hat.

1

and grandpa goat

2

Horse says, "Hi."

2

go over the gate.

Hippo says, "Hi."

Good-bye goats.

4

Hippo hugs horse.

4

I read my
Little Book to:

1. _____

2. _____

3. _____

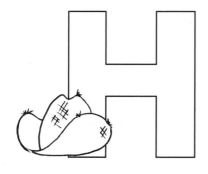

I read my
Little Book to:

1. _____

2. _____

3. _____

My Little **I** Book

My Little **J** Book

Ink on ivy.

1

Jack and Jill.

1

Ink on igloo.

2

Jack juggles

2

Ink on ice cream.

3

and Jill jumps

3

Icky ink!

4

on a jeep.

4

I read my
Little Book to:

1. _____

2. _____

3. _____

I read my
Little Book to:

1. _____

2. _____

3. _____

My Little K Book

KING

Book

My Little L Book

Book

King kisses.

Lamb licks

2

King kicks.

2

and lion licks.

3 **King carries**

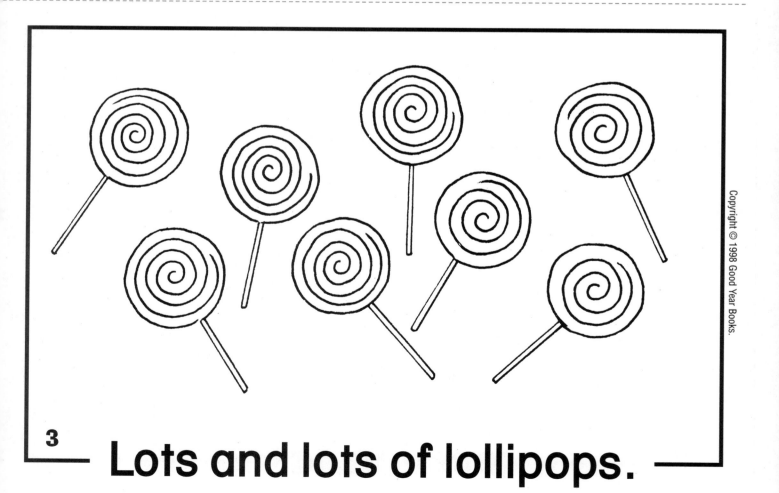

3 **Lots and lots of lollipops.**

a kitty-cat.

Lucky lamb and lion.

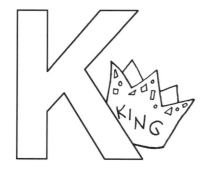

I read my
Little Book to:

1. _____

2. _____

3. _____

I read my
Little Book to:

1. _____

2. _____

3. _____

My
Little M
Book

My
Little N

Book

Monsters mixing.

1

Nine in a nest.

1

Monsters mopping.

2

Naptime!

Nanny says, "Nap time."

2

3

Messy monsters

3

Nine say, "No."

and me in the middle.

4

Nanny says, "Now!"

4

M

I read my
Little Book to:

1. _____

2. _____

3. _____

N

I read my
Little Book to:

1. _____

2. _____

3. _____

My Little O Book

My Little P Book

1 **Otter over ostrich.**

1 **Pig and pretzels.**

Otter on ostrich.

2

Pig and peanuts.

2

3 Otter off ostrich.

3 Pot of potatoes.

Ouch!

4

Pigs at a picnic.

4

O I read my
Little Book to:

1. _____

2. _____

3. _____

P I read my
Little Book to:

1. _____

2. _____

3. _____

My Little **Q** Book

My Little **R** Book

1

Quack, quack, quack.

1

Rabbit with a rose

Quiet!

"Quiet", says the queen.

2

and robin with a rose

2

3

Quack, quack, quack.

3

run in the rain,

"Quiet! Quit quacking."

4

reaching the rainbow.

4

I read my
Little Book to:

1. _____

2. _____

3. _____

I read my
Little Book to:

1. _____

2. _____

3. _____

My Little **S** Book

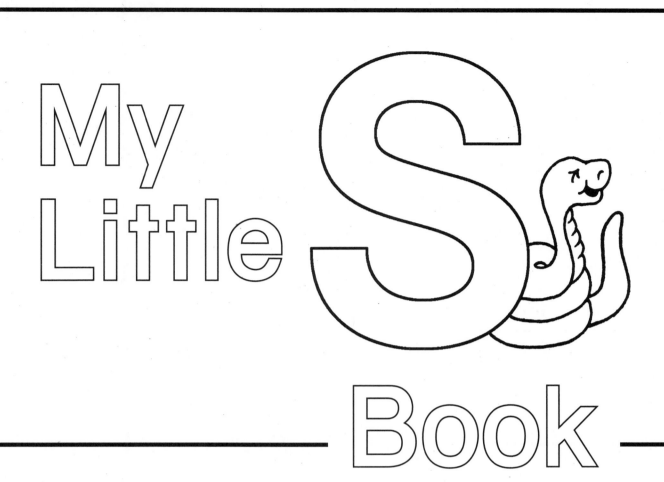

My Little **T** Book

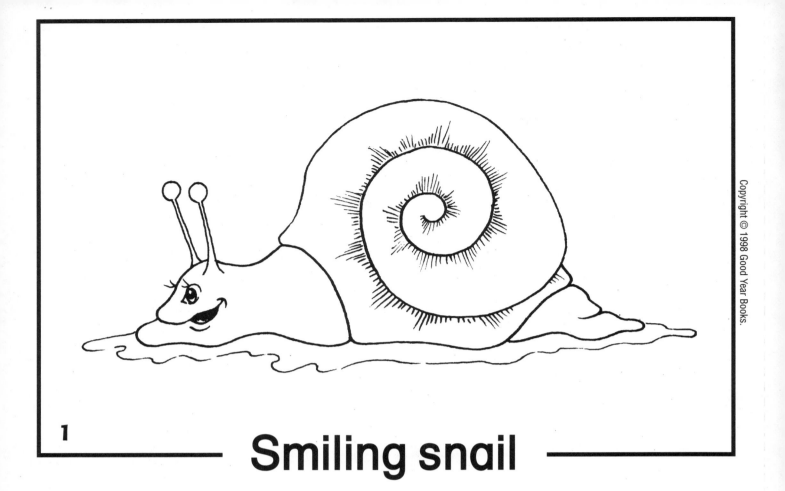

1

Smiling snail

1

Teeny-tiny tiger

and smiling snake 2

and teeny-tiny turtle 2

3

and smiling spider

3

take a trip

sail on soap. **4**

on a teeny-tiny train. **4**

 I read my
Little Book to:

1. _____

2. _____

3. _____

 I read my
Little Book to:

1. _____

2. _____

3. _____

My Little **U** Book

My Little **V** Book

Umbrella is up.

1

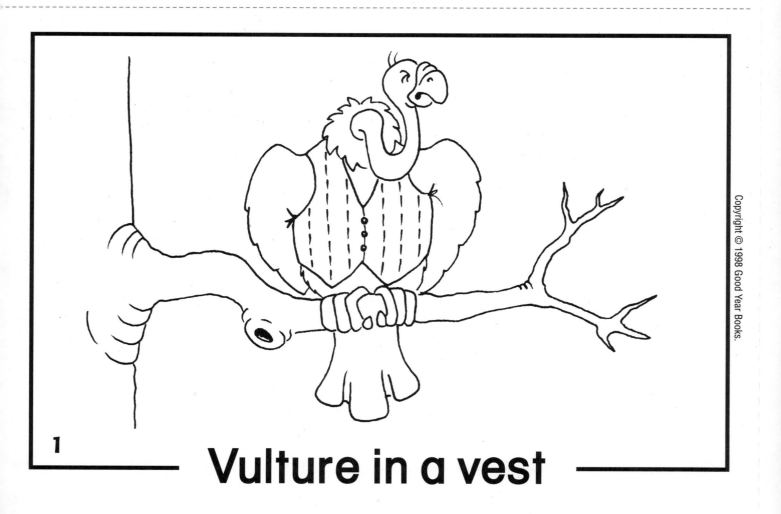

Vulture in a vest

1

Umpire under umbrella.

2

over a volcano.

2

3

Uh-oh!

3

VOOSH!

Upside-down umbrella.

4

Vulture has vanished.

4

I read my
Little Book to:

1. _____

2. _____

3. _____

I read my
Little Book to:

1. _____

2. _____

3. _____

My Little ____ W Book

My Little ____ X Book

1 Winking whale

1 X-ray the fox.

and winking walrus

2

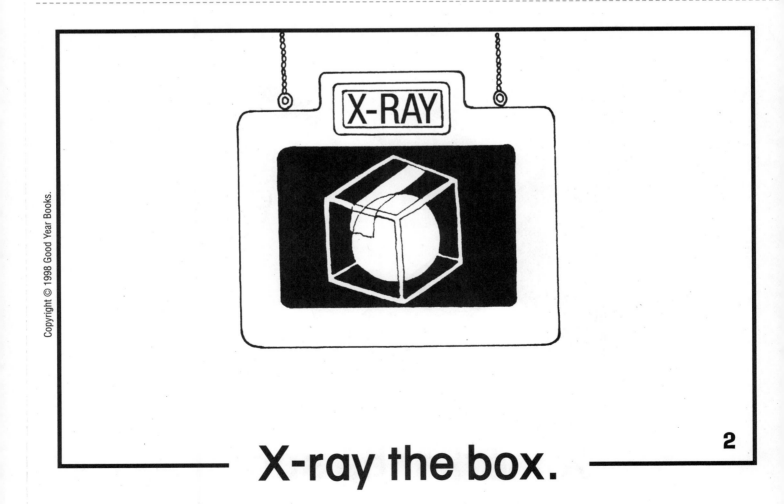

X-RAY

X-ray the box.

2

3

wear wigs

3

X marks the spot

in the water.

4

to X-ray the ox.

4

W I read my
Little Book to:

1. _____

2. _____

3. _____

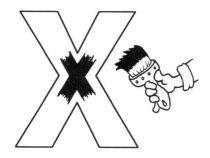

X I read my
Little Book to:

1. _____

2. _____

3. _____

My
Little **Y**

Book

My
Little **Z**

Book

1

Yak yawns.

1

Zebra in the zoo.

Yak yells,

2

Zebra zips his zipper.

2

"Where's my yogurt?"

3

Zebra zigs and zags

3

Yogurt is yummy!

4

ZOO

out of the zoo.

4

I read my
Little Book to:

1. _____

2. _____

3. _____

I read my
Little Book to:

1. _____

2. _____

3. _____